4-7-10

God Bless You.

Barbara Arbuckle

Life Lessons from the Little Ones

Words, Wit, and Wisdom Reflect God's Great Love

Barbara Arbuckle

Copyright © 2009 by Barbara Desenberg Arbuckle

All rights reserved. No part of this book shall be reproduced or transmitted in any form or by any means, electronic, mechanical, magnetic, photographic including photocopying, recording or by any information storage and retrieval system, without prior written permission of the publisher. No patent liability is assumed with respect to the use of the information contained herein. Although every precaution has been taken in the preparation of this book, the publisher and author assume no responsibility for errors or omissions. Neither is any liability assumed for damages resulting from the use of the information contained herein.

ISBN 0-7414-5592-7

Published by:

INFI∞ITY
PUBLISHING.COM

1094 New DeHaven Street, Suite 100
West Conshohocken, PA 19428-2713
Info@buybooksontheweb.com
www.buybooksontheweb.com
Toll-free (877) BUY BOOK
Local Phone (610) 941-9999
Fax (610) 941-9959

Printed in the United States of America

Published September 2009

DEDICATION

- ♥ To Dad for his great love of life and of family.

- ♥ To Mom for unconditional love and for always being there to listen.

- ♥ To Jim, my husband and my best friend. We met in high school and are celebrating 35 extraordinary years. Thank you.

- ♥ To Julie, my daughter, who has always been the strongest support in my life and words cannot do her justice.

- ♥ To Jamie, my son, whose gentleness and vivacious love of life and the outdoors inspires me so.

- ♥ To David, my son-in-law, who teaches us to be our best and gives great love and support to his family.

- ♥ To Colin, my grandson, who melts my heart with his smile.

I would like to thank Matt Pinto and Lorraine Ranalli for their assistance and guidance in writing this book.

Unless you change and become like little children, says the Lord, you shall not enter the Kingdom of Heaven (Matt 18:3).

Contents

Introduction i
Be a Peacemaker 1
Don't Give Up 5
Be Patient 7
Simply Listen 9
Trust Like a Child 13
The Miracle of Friendship 15
From the Mouths of Babes… 17
Be Kind 21
Love Can Carry You Through 29
The Power of Prayer 31
Think Before You Speak 33
Respect Everyone 35
Be Humble 37
Help is There, Just Ask 39
Sing a Simple Song 41
Use Your Imagination 43
Think of Others 45
Go with the Flow 47
Spend Time with the Special People in Your Life ... 49
Care About Our World 51

Dream 55
Give from the Heart 57
Faith Gives Us Hope 59

INTRODUCTION

Between my 30 years of motherhood and my 16 years experience as a Catholic School Kindergarten Teacher, I learned that only in God is my soul at rest. Simply put, He is my strength and my hope. Despite having heard it countless times in homilies and private discussions, I finally have come to accept from the depths of my soul that God truly is love. *Whoever is without love does not know God, for God is love* (1 John 4:8). I also realized that as unimaginable as it may seem, the God of the Universe actually speaks to us when we silence our hearts and listen. His message always fills us with peace and hope.

In 2006, I made the tough decision to retire from teaching. I had wrestled with this option because my teaching years were some of the best and most blessed times of my life. The grace I received far exceeded the salary I was paid. Little blessings were practically a daily occurrence for me, and those I cherished most were the bits of wisdom that came from the tender, often whimsical and usually rambunctious, five-year-olds in my care.

Soon after retiring from the kindergarten at St. Maximilian Kolbe School in West Chester, Pennsylvania, I broke open a collection of funny phrases and profound gems that I had saved. Some are words of hope, others reflect sadness, struggles, joy, and laughter, but each is rooted in God's love and each was delivered to me from Him through the mouths of babes.

So, I share these gems with you and I pray that you, too, will be touched, as I was, and inspired, as I am, to stop, listen, and allow God's love to enter your heart. In a world rife with techno-gizmos and gadgets we often need to be reminded to make time for meditation.

The beauty of these simple passages, and my humble reflections that follow, is that none of us need a degree in theology to understand or to relate. We just need to be open to God's greatest mysteries and truths of life. Each story is followed by my interpretation of the message, the wisdom to guide us, and the action we can incorporate into our lives. God speaks to us all the time, often through unexpected voices.

BE A PEACEMAKER

"If I was the President, I would be a peacemaker and feed the poor."

One year, in celebration of Presidents' Day, I instructed my students to cut a silhouette of George Washington out of construction paper. When they were through, I had them close their eyes and imagine for a moment that they were the president of the United States. "What would you do?" I asked. Looking around the room, I noticed a variety of expressions. With eyes closed, the darlings seemed pensive. Intense thinking furrowed some brows, while other faces seemed relaxed by peaceful thoughts. After a short while, I had them open their eyes and illustrate their thoughts on scrap paper.

Following the activity, we discussed ways to make the world a better place. Each child enthusiastically shared his or her version of peace. Ryan, an energetic fair-haired boy with an adorably freckled face, was the kind of kid who entered the classroom as though each day was his first. Sporting a toothless smile, he explained the importance of remembering people who have no home.

Steven, who always exhibited a special sense of selflessness, shot up and announced that he'd like to give his life savings to the poor. "If I was the president," he said earnestly, "I would be a peacemaker and feed the poor." Steven's words were simple but the tenderness with which his eyes spoke struck a nerve in me. Most of the children I taught knew material comforts as I did; yet I could imagine this little boy walking cold desolate streets to feed the poor.

At a committee meeting a few days later, my principal made a comment that reminded me of my President's Day experience. She said that like adults, children can donate money and material items but until they actually spend time with the less fortunate, they cannot fully comprehend poverty.

After retiring, I came to fully understand that concept when I began taking my mother to a nearby Day Room that feeds the poor. I could not hold back my tears as I witnessed one poverty stricken person after another. Each was cloaked with a distressing background, yet each beamed with joyfulness not because they were getting a meal but because they were getting attention from other human beings. Why is it that the easiest sacrifice—time and attention—is the most difficult to part with?

Although I get choked up at the Day Room, and I was especially tearful during my first visit, the experience is so indescribably gratifying and fulfilling that I look forward to going back. I am convinced that there is no gift greater than that of giving. Seeing so many people who suffer in so many ways come together to offer heartfelt thanks in prayer before their meal is truly a beautiful sight to behold.

The Message: Steven's simple words echoed in my mind a few years later when I read this classic prayer from Mother Teresa:

> *The fruit of silence is prayer*
> *The fruit of prayer is faith*
> *The fruit of faith is love*
> *The fruit of love is service*
> *The fruit of service is peace*

I've always been inspired by the work of Mother Teresa, a woman who surrendered her will to God's will. She tended to the poorest of poor and offered sincere love for the dying when no one else was there.

The Wisdom: *Lord, make me an instrument of Thy peace;*
where there is hatred, let me sow love;
where there is injury, pardon;
where there is doubt, faith;
where there is despair, hope;
where there is darkness, light;
and where there is sadness, joy.
O Divine Master,
grant that I may not so much seek to be consoled as to console;
to be understood, as to understand;
to be loved, as to love;
for it is in giving that we receive,
it is in pardoning that we are pardoned,
and it is in dying that we are born to Eternal Life.
– Prayer of St. Francis

The Action: Be a peacemaker today. When a conflict arises at home or at work, choose to remain silent, consciously loving the "other" as you would want them to love and honor you.

DON'T GIVE UP

"I can't write stories, I speak Spanish."

My grade partner introduced me to a writing process called Kid Writing, a systematic approach to help children write. I attended workshops, read and reread materials, and enthusiastically used the methods in my classroom for years. With each passing year, I became increasingly amazed by the ability of these five-year-olds.

I distinctly remember causing a stir with one class. Every student looked at me as if I were in the wrong room or maybe even the wrong school when I explained during our first week together the writing accomplishments we could expect to complete by the end of the school year. I began with my usual dialogue, "Each of us is precious and we all have many wonderful stories to tell. By the springtime, we will have *written* many of these stories." As twenty puzzled faces stared back at me, some with heads cocked to one side like puppy dogs, I continued with words of encouragement, "I know each of you is capable of doing extraordinary things and I'm going to be here every day to help you."

Our daily routine included morning writing lessons. In addition, we set aside four special times each week for journal writing, which was a three-step process. Parents helped with these sessions on a rotating basis. First, the children were to illustrate the story they wanted to tell. Then, they had to discuss their picture with a parent volunteer or with me. We helped the children organize their thoughts before they began writing. When it came time for writing, step three, children were instructed to sound out the words they wanted to use and to simply place a "magic line" where they were not sure of a letter. When they were through, the parents and I praised the children's work, reviewed it with them, and wrote the correct spelling at the bottom of their pages.

Because English was one little girl's second language she was very intimidated. Picking up on this, I encouraged Maria to draw additional pictures in order to express herself. Eventually, she developed a sequence to her stories through pictures. It was thrilling to observe Maria's determination as she communicated in a comfortable fashion. Before long, her confidence increased and translated seamlessly to her verbal explanations, and then into her writing.

Maria's writing had become quite good. So good, in fact, that I read her stories to the class and watched as the excitement spread. By the end of the year, Maria and another little girl had so many stories written that I decided to bring the two of them to a teachers' workshop. My colleagues were utterly impressed by the accomplishments of these two kindergartners.

The Message: Encouragement and support are the mortar that bonds guided instruction and performance to form a solid foundation of confidence.

The Wisdom: *Encourage each other everyday* (Hebrews 3:13).

The Action: Like anything else, confidence begets confidence. Walk with an attitude of faith and determination so that others may be inspired by your example.

BE PATIENT

"My Mom asked her boss at work to be patient because she wanted to come to our Mother's Day Celebration."

Excited that the long-awaited celebration day was finally here, Liam blurted that little tidbit of information upon entering the classroom one Friday in May. Patience was not a new concept to Liam; he had heard that word plenty of times in my classroom as we prepared for this very day. One by one, each student entered the room with a bit more anticipation than usual on the morning of our Mother's Day Tea.

A month of preparation preceded that very special day. We painted pictures of our moms, made bookmarks, strung brightly colored beads on elastic string to make bracelets, and made hats decorated with tissue paper flowers. Our biggest accomplishment, however, was our handwritten books about what makes Mom so special.

Each time we completed a craft, at least one child said that he or she couldn't wait to give it to his or her mother. My aide and I constantly reminded the children that they had to be patient. Needless to say, the children were bursting at the seams waiting to reveal their surprise.

Our classroom was impeccably neat that morning, and to set the mood, we had the gentle and melodic sounds of a harp playing softly in the background as the mothers entered the room. Upon arrival, each mother received a hug and a handmade flower from her child, who then escorted her to her personally decorated seat. Each child sat on his or her mother's lap as my aide and I took turns reading the loving and humorous tributes to Mom. Practically experts in the art of patience at this point, the children waited graciously to hear their own stories, and they lit with joy and clapped heartily after hearing their classmates' stories.

Children respond remarkably well to our expectations. I can recall being surprised and delighted by the effort that went into a hand-stitched heart that my own daughter had given me one Mother's Day. She displayed diligence in not only making the craft, but also in patiently waiting to present it. At a relatively young age, but not kindergarten, my son dug out a section of my garden to install a pond. Again, the joy we both experienced had more to do with the effort and patience involved than with the finished product, although it was impressive.

The Message: Good things come to those who wait. It may sound trite and cliché, but it is so true.

The Wisdom: *Put on then, as God's chosen ones, holy and beloved, heartfelt compassion, kindness, humility, gentleness, and patience.* (Colossians 3:12).

The Action: When waiting feels more like an exercise in tedium, we have to remind ourselves to place our trust and reliance on the Lord, for He truly does reward perseverance.

Also, learn to prioritize, to put ancillary things on hold when our loved ones need us. The important things in life aren't things, but people.

SIMPLY LISTEN

"Everybody is so busy in my house. Nobody listens to me."

The Terrible Thing That Happened at My House is a story about a little girl who was very content with life until her mother took a job. Life, as the girl knew it, had been turned completely upside down. Evenings—once a time for relaxed conversation—had become a time of controlled mayhem with hurried chores and frantic preparation for the next day. The girl felt lost in the shuffle, abandoned.

I decided to read this story following a conversation with a mother who had sought my help because she was having a difficult time with her oldest daughter, Ava. Strong-willed and domineering, Ava was becoming increasingly disruptive at home, to the point where she was bossing her younger siblings around as if she were their mother. Overwhelmed and at her wits end, Ava's mother had hoped that an example in the classroom would inspire Ava to reflect on her behavior.

After reading the story I asked my students if they ever felt like the little girl. As I suspected, and dreaded, they related all too well. Isn't it sad that our lives have become so hectic that we barely hear or notice one another?

In the last half century, our society has evolved into a hasty smorgasbord of to-do lists, super-sized everything and wrapped to go. Sure, my father, like most, was busy trying to earn a living, and he traveled a lot. But there was an order, a routine, in our house and in most of the households in the twentieth century. Despite his business obligations, my father always reserved one week each year for our family vacation. Regardless where we went or what we did, vacation was an extra special time because the whole family was together, uninterrupted, for seven straight days.

Our annual retreats may seem dull by today's standards but they generated some of our fondest memories. One summer, we hiked about 14,000 feet up the side of a mountain in the Canadian Rockies. After eight hours of climbing we sat quietly on boulders and simply took in the magnificent view. What a treat it was to see birds glide against the backdrop of majestic mountain ranges through the still late afternoon air. The awesomeness of God and His creation was ever-present in the serenity of that moment. We could hear His voice in the quiet and it made us feel secure. Years later, as my father lay dying, I held his hand and thanked him for providing that breathtaking experience.

Mom, on the other hand, was almost always there to listen. It was rare that women of her generation worked outside the home. My siblings and I agree that we were quite blessed to have been raised at such a time, and we regret that we have not always been able to afford the same gift to our children.

Reflecting on my own childhood, I was not at all surprised by the almost instantaneous conclusion of one of our school counselors regarding Ava. She recommended more one-on-one time between Ava and her mother. To what extent, if any, *The Terrible Thing That Happened at My House* impacted Ava, we may never know. But Ava's mother did report a dramatic change in her daughter's behavior after she made a conscious effort to pay closer attention to her.

The Message: Listening is the better part of communication. We benefit more from listening to others than from voicing our concerns.

The Wisdom: *God told Elijah to meet Him at the mountain. Elijah waited. There was a mighty windstorm, an earthquake, a fire but the Lord wasn't in any of these. He came to Elijah in a gentle whisper* (1 Kings 19:11).

The Action: Listen. Perhaps God gave us two ears and one mouth so we can listen twice as much as we speak.

TRUST LIKE A CHILD

"If you're upset about your dog, just think how I feel because my mom died."

Morning Circle was a time when the students and I gathered to share concerns and events going on in our lives. With legs crossed, we would sit in a big circle on a carpeted area in the classroom. I shared as well.

One year, I had been keeping the children abreast of my dog's failing health. When the day had come to break the sad news that Fluffy passed away, I was mentally prepared to respond to the children's sorrow but I was ill prepared for my own reaction. I began to cry as I relayed the news.

Michael, who had lost his mother prior to the start of the school year, raised his hand immediately. I was made aware of Michael's loss over the summer but we had not discussed it in class up to that point. When I nodded toward him, he began to explain how he understood sadness. He told the class that his mom watches over him from Heaven. He said that just as God was taking care of his mom, He was taking care of Fluffy, too. Michael assured us that although we were sad, we did not need to worry.

Michael's testimonial drew silence from the classroom. The children and I sat frozen in time as we reflected on his words of wisdom. What a gift Michael was at a time when everyone in the class was reminded of some sort of loss they had experienced. Could little five-year-old Michael have known the cathartic affect he had on us? As difficult as it was to lose his Mom, the way Michael trusted without question was an inspiration that surpassed his understanding.

The Message: Rather than questioning like an adult, sometimes it is necessary to trust like a child.

The Wisdom: *With all your heart you must trust the Lord and not your own judgment. Always let Him lead you, and He will clear the road for you to follow* (Proverbs 3:5-6).

The Action: Accept everything with submission to God's will. –Mother Teresa

THE MIRACLE OF FRIENDSHIP

"Look outside! It's snowing miracles."

Despite extensive surgery, Josh's vision was far from perfect. He had been through five eye operations by the time he reached Kindergarten but Josh's impairment did not hinder his energy. His concept of distance was askew, so he often bumped into things. Behind Josh's coke-bottle glasses everyone could see a dogged zest for life in his eyes. It was not unusual to hear "Josh, slow down" or "Walk, Josh" from a teacher or administrator as Josh ran through the main school doors each morning.

Failing to heed the daily warning, Josh ran in from the schoolyard after recess one afternoon and collided head first with a bookshelf. Head wounds are quite horrific looking and Josh's was no exception. The site of blood gushing sent some children scattering and drew others closer. Each of us was shaken. By the grace of God, Josh was all right, but it was a tough lesson learned for him and for the rest of the class.

Josh was going to have to take it easy—a concept that may have made him uncomfortable because of the possible social ramifications. After all, five-year-old boys do not "take it easy." I often wondered whether his energy was a subconscious means of overcompensating for his poor eyesight.

Children can be cruel, but we were fortunate that this bunch encouraged Josh heartily, especially Christopher. I watched their friendship bud. Josh had little interest in writing and drawing until he started to exchange notes with his new friend. As his trust increased, Josh confided in Christopher about his fear of playing ball with the others. Christopher said, "That's OK. We'll have a catch, just you and me."

So each day they tossed a ball back and forth until Josh felt comfortable enough to join the rest of the class. By the end of the school year, no one could discern which was the rookie.

In January, Josh was the first student to notice the year's first snowfall. "Look outside," he said, "it's snowing miracles." "You're a miracle," I thought to myself, having witnessed first-hand the speed of trust. For Josh did settle down once his confidence had increased. It didn't happen over night but over the course of an extraordinary school year, with help and attention from an extraordinary friend.

The Message: When someone believes in you, your world changes in a positive way.

The Wisdom: *A faithful friend is a sturdy shelter: he who finds one finds a treasure* (Sirach 6:14).

The Action: Knowing we have support makes us feel secure and when we feel secure we are confident. Be a trustworthy friend and make a sincere effort to show support. Then, watch your friend or loved one's quality of life increase at the rate their confidence increases.

FROM THE MOUTHS OF BABES…..

"My dad did not sign me up for rest time."

> I had three children in my classroom named Matthew. Not thinking one day, I simply called out, "Matthew." A little girl replied, "What kind of Matthew do you want?"

As I prepared the children for dismissal, one child called out, "OK kids; the show is over."

> "My sister had a cold and she hatched it on me."

As I wiped a table after snack time one day, I remarked, "Boy, there sure are a lot of crumbs at this table." Without hesitation, a little girl replied, "That's because we were eating crummy food."

A boy told the class about the big birthday celebration his family had had for his grandfather. "He is either 73 or 37. I don't remember."

"I met a bear in the woods and we have lots of fun together but don't check on this with my mom because she won't know anything about it."

"No one is going to listen to you today with your hair looking like that."

Commenting on my hand-stitched brightly colored sweater, a student approached me and said, "That is a sweater a grandmother would like."

On a field trip a girl asked one of the dad's who was chaperoning, "Please carry my lunch bag, because when I carry it, it gives me a headache."

Following an Easter egg hunt a little girl asked her friend if she collected many eggs. "Yes," she replied, "I collected a many."

"My cat brings home the cutest dead mice."

The Message: Laughter is the best medicine.

The Wisdom: *A cheerful heart is good medicine* (Proverbs 17:22).

The Action: Laugh.

BE KIND

"It really is all about being nice to other people, isn't it?"

With a pensive look in her eyes, Kiera asked that rhetorical question as she flung her little backpack over one shoulder and passed through the threshold at the end of the school day. "Yes," I responded softly, "It's all about being nice."

I had been encouraging the children to notice random acts of kindness that occur automatically in our classroom but are often taken for granted. I pointed to examples as they happened and the children beamed with excitement over the attention. I made special note of how Alicia didn't think twice about picking up Jimmy's pencil after it rolled off of his desk.

I congratulated the entire class for taking it upon themselves to make finding Janine's hat their mission. She had come in from recess crying over the missing hat.

When I returned to school following a two-day absence due to a nasty head cold, the children were extremely nurturing. They handed me tissues and the get-well cards that they had made. They asked if I was OK. And one child even offered to get the school nurse.

The recognition of such acts had a positive impact on two levels. Each student felt a bit more self-assured and each was inspired to do more for their classmates.

I asked the children, "Have you ever felt warm and fuzzy inside?" There was a collective, "Ooh" as hands went up across the classroom. I pointed to Mark who said, "I know, like when you do something for someone and you can see that it really made them happy." Other children nodded in agreement. We briefly went around the room and heard comments such as, "My mother made me feel warm and fuzzy inside when she hugged me because I walked the dog without being told to do so," and "Yeah, my mom high-fived me after I put my empty milk glass in the dishwasher."

I told the children that I think the warm and fuzzy feeling comes from an invisible thermometer that God put inside us. When we are kind, the temperature rises inside us and we feel warm and beam with energy. When we are mean, the temperature plummets and we are cold and cranky, and worse yet, others see the coldness in our hearts.

The Message: Kindness begets kindness.

The Wisdom: *Kind words can be short and easy to speak, but their echoes are truly endless.* –Mother Teresa

The Action: Set out to change the world one random act of kindness at a time.

Life Lessons From the Little Ones

My parents with my husband and children.

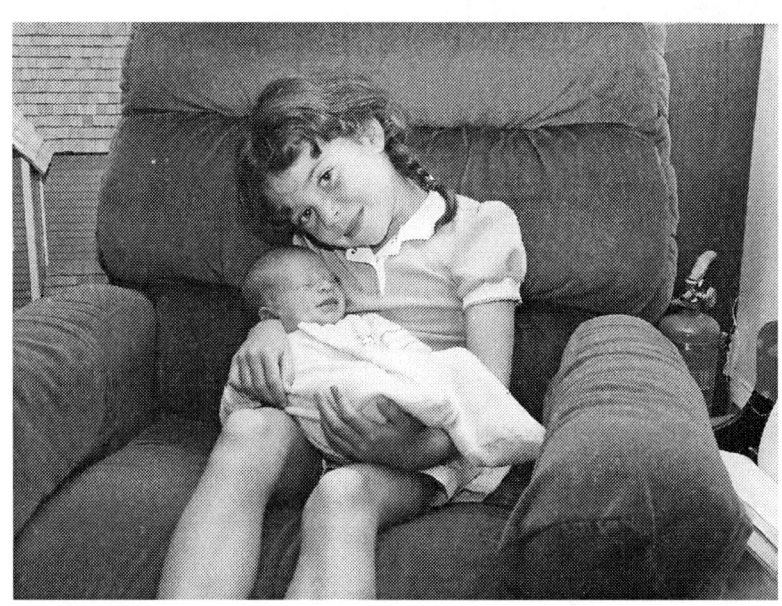

My daughter, Julie, welcomes her new brother, Jamie.

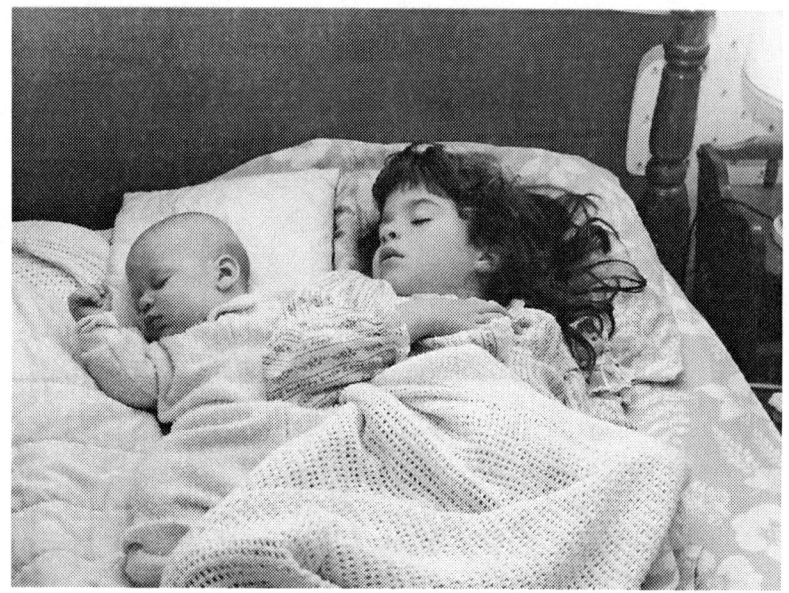

My peaceful children.

Our family on a vacation.

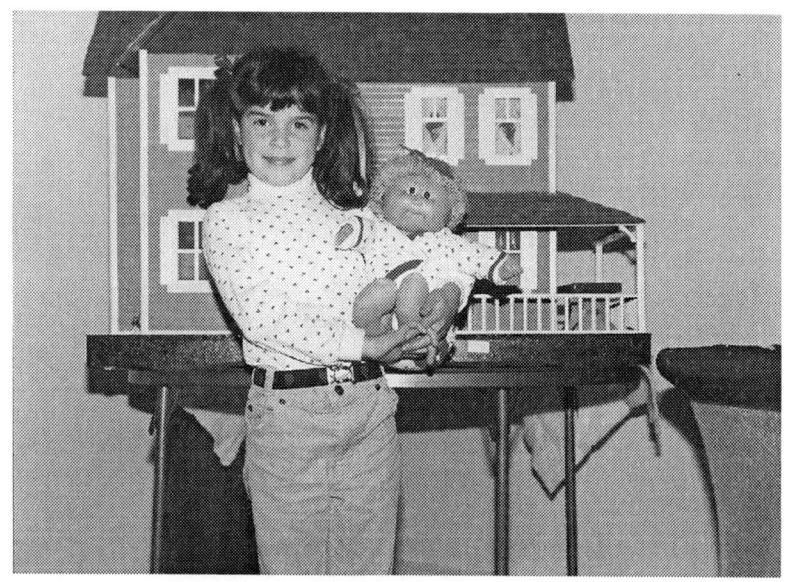

Julie always notices the details and made sure her doll had a matching shirt.

Jamie showing his love of the outdoors.

My husband teaching our children about caring for God's creatures.

Our family of four.

Jamie has a gentle and caring way.

Julie with my son-in-law, Dave, with their son, Colin.

My husband is my best friend.

My mom and I love to spend time with Colin.

LOVE CAN CARRY YOU THROUGH

"My mom said, if I put my hand on my heart, I will know that she is thinking of me and she loves me."

The first day of school elicits a bagful of emotions from students, parents, and teachers alike—anxiety, fear, anticipation, sadness, and happiness, just to name a few. With new faces, classrooms, buildings, rules, and expectations, the adjustments can be overwhelming and cause some students to cry. This is especially true for kindergartners, and especially those enrolled in a full-day program. For many, it's their very first school experience. It's no wonder so many long for the comforts of home.

To help the children adjust to their first day away from mom and dad, I plan a heap of activities. I find that it not only keeps them involved and interested, but also makes the day go a little quicker. My plan was foiled one year when Sean kept retreating to his desk in an attempt to isolate himself from the others. The first time, I let him be for a few minutes, but I called him over when I was about to take the students outside to introduce them to the playground. Sean walked behind the others. With his chin pointed downward, his eyes peered shyly through the straight black bangs that dangled in front of them.

When we reentered the classroom, Sean slipped back into seclusion, sitting with his arms crossed and his feet curled beneath his legs as though he were cuddling himself. I walked over and, leaning into him, I asked if he was OK. He said that he loved his mom so much and that she loved him, too. She had told him that whenever he felt lonely and missed her all he had to do was place his hand over his heart to be reminded of her deep love for him and to be comforted.

"Wow! What a wonderful plan," I responded. With my hand on his shoulder, I said, "You go right ahead and do that whenever you need to, and then come back and join us. OK?" He shook his head and looking up at me with a smile on his face, I could see that he was relieved.

Every once in a while, Sean would break away from the group and head back to his seat. As the year progressed, he did this less and less. By Halloween, he had stopped doing it completely. Knowing he could keep his mom close to him, Sean was not only able to get through his day, but also enjoy it.

The Message: Our words can bring great comfort to those we love.

The Wisdom: *Follow the way of love* (Corinthians 14:1).

The Action: Don't assume that your loved ones know how you feel about them. Remind them frequently. Three little words—I love you—can have an enormous impact.

THE POWER OF PRAYER

"I heard the news last night. There was a plane that crashed into two buildings. People were hurt. I think we should pray for peace."

Everyone remembers where they were and the emotions they felt as the news unfolded on September 11, 2001. I had just left my class with the gym teacher and stopped by the school office to check my mailbox. Our secretary told me that a plane crashed into one of the towers at the World Trade Center. A feeling of horror came over me as a thousand images flashed through my mind. I had left the office before the news came across about the second plane, but for some reason, I had a strange suspicion that this was no mere accident. Given the little I know about flight patterns and Air Traffic Control, the crash defied any logical explanation.

Like everyone else, I did not understand what was going on but I was upset. I began to pray. It was all I could do to remain calm. While waiting for the students to return, I selected a few fun storybooks from one of the shelves in my classroom. I figured that reading the books would distract me, and the children if they had heard anything in passing, from news of this horrible disaster.

At 9:15, I returned to the gym to pick up my students. When we got back to our classroom we found several frightened parents waiting to take their children out of school for the day. In a hushed manner, some of the parents relayed the news to me about the second plane. My stomach sank as I realized that my instincts had been confirmed. The children were also getting wind that our country was in some sort of imminent danger. Since so many parents were trickling in to pick up their little ones, I decided to let the children play rather than listen to me read. First, however, I asked the children and parents to join me in prayer. We prayed, as we did each day, for peace.

The following day, the children came to school very anxious, buzzing about the news and sharing their interpretations. During Morning Circle, I let each of the children relieve their worries. When everyone had a chance to speak, I complimented them on their compassion and terrific suggestions on how to avoid conflict and move forward. I also applauded them for wanting to help the victims and families that had been devastated by this atrocity. "We all know how good we feel when we are helping others, but what's the one way we can help right now, right from our circle?" I asked. As the others pondered my question, Cynthia raised her hand tentatively. "Pray?" She said. "Yes, we can turn to God." "Yeah," Gregory exclaimed, "He'll know what to do."

We joined our hands together and asked God to help everyone in our school, our homes, our communities, our country, and across the globe get past this tragedy. We prayed for the repose of the souls of each and every victim. We prayed for peace.

The Message: Sometimes prayer is the only help we can offer, and that's OK.

The Wisdom: *Prayer feeds the soul; as blood is to the body, prayer is to the soul and it brings us closer to God.* –Mother Teresa

The Action: Rely on God. After all, He invites us to do so.

THINK BEFORE YOU SPEAK

"I shouldn't have said that, it was mean."

I found Elizabeth standing alone crying in the recess yard. When I asked her why she was crying she said that Sarah had hurt her. "Where does it hurt?" I asked. Pointing to her heart, Elizabeth said, "Right here." It hadn't dawned on me that the hurt was emotional. "Do you want to tell me what happened?" "Well," she said, "Sarah, told me I can't play with the other girls because I look different."

As human nature dictates, some of us are leaders and others are followers. For whatever reason, Sarah had become the girl that all the others looked up to. Unfortunately, Sarah did not know how to properly handle that responsibility.

Inconspicuously, I guided the two girls onto a nearby bench for a brief discussion. I told Sarah that she hurt Elizabeth and asked her if she had any idea how. She lowered her head and admitted that she had told Elizabeth that she couldn't play with the rest of the girls because she was different. "I appreciate your honesty, Sarah. It takes a lot of courage to own up to our actions," I added. Then I asked her how she would feel in Elizabeth's shoes. Sarah began to cry.

I turned to Elizabeth and said, "Sometimes we make mistakes and say things we regret. Will you forgive Sarah?" Elizabeth looked at Sarah and said, "I forgive you." Sarah cried a bit harder. I asked Sarah if she realized how the others looked to her as a leader. She did. "Even leaders make mistakes," I explained. "Strong leaders acknowledge their mistakes and set things right. They look out for everyone."

Sarah dried her eyes, looked directly at Elizabeth, and then hugged her. "Please come and play with us," Sarah said. And Elizabeth did.

Sarah never lost her innate leadership qualities. Over the years, I caught glimpses of her in the schoolyard, or heard other teachers make complimentary remarks about her. She was a true leader, always looking out for the underdog, which unbeknown to her garnered increased respect from her classmates.

The Message: Actions speak louder than words, and when harsh words accompany inconsiderate actions, the affect can be devastating.

The Wisdom: *When you talk, do not say harmful things but say what people need; words that will help others become stronger* (Ephesians 4:29).

The Action: Choose words carefully and be even more conscientious about actions.

RESPECT EVERYONE

"But my skin is a different color than the other kids."

Every January I hung a poster of Martin Luther King, Jr. in my classroom. I taught the children about his accomplishments and I described how people of color were once segregated in our country. Children are always shocked to learn that our government once required Blacks to drink from different water fountains than Whites, had separate schools for Black children, and didn't allow Black people to vote. The children just couldn't comprehend such cold-heartedness. I suspected that some doubted what I was teaching was true.

While visiting my daughter in New York City one spring, I had an opportunity to meet an EWTN personality after Mass at St. Patrick's Cathedral. I had always been a fan of hers, so I sought her advice on teaching students about the injustices of our country's past. I explained that I wanted the children to learn from these mistakes. She advised me to focus on the accomplishments of all those who shaped our country's history, Black and White, and to not dwell on the negatives.

When, for the first time, I had an African-American student in my class, I quickly discovered that teaching with this approach was beneficial to students of all nationalities. During a typical Morning Circle, I was explaining the immensity of God's love for each of us; how each child is precious in God's eyes. That's when Evan raised his hand to say, "But my skin is a different color than the other kids." "Yes, Evan it is," I said "But if you look around, no two of us are exactly alike. We know that as Creator, God is all-powerful. Right?" They all nodded. "Well God is all-knowing too. In fact, He knows each of us down to the number of hairs on our heads. And each of us is special and unique in God's eyes."

Another tool I use in the classroom is *Sister Ann's Hands*, a beautiful book about a nun who, upon learning that a child was going to be taken out of the school because her parents didn't want their little girl to be taught by a Black nun, tenderly taught her students to judge people by their hearts and not their skin color. I noticed that after reading the book to my class, it was regularly checked out from our school library.

The Message: "Different" does not mean better or worse; it is simply a way to describe "unique."

The Wisdom: *Love each other with genuine affection and take delight in honoring each other* (Romans 12:10).

The Action: Hold fast to Martin Luther King's dream and ask God to soften the hearts of all men.

BE HUMBLE

"Those girls over there think that I know everything and I don't."

Have you ever noticed how competitive young children can be? They love to boast about their accomplishments. "I can ride a two-wheeler." "I stayed up until 11:00 last night." "I lost two teeth this week." "Well, I've already lost three." The list goes on. Children often develop a sense of who they are and opinions about each other based on these very base events. This is how misconceptions form. Unfortunately, adults are often victims and perpetrators of similar misconceptions. Like adults, children as young as five notice the cars people drive, types of houses in which they live, clothes they wear, and friends they keep.

Laura, a very bright student who read fluently before she entered Kindergarten, seemed to always have the answers. It was not unusual to hear Laura shout out rules to a game or call out directions in the recess yard. She felt it was her appointed duty to direct the class' playtime, and the other students seemed to comply without question.

Kathleen, on the other hand, struggled academically. So, imagine my surprise when I found Kathleen teaching Laura how to tie her shoes. The girls had not noticed my gaze. Later, however, when I found Kathleen teaching Laura sign language, I complimented Kathleen on her skillfulness. That was when Laura turned to me and said, "Those girls over there think that I know everything and I don't." At that moment I realized that I was guilty, too. I had underestimated Laura's humility. She had been getting weary of the pressure of being everyone's go-to person.

The following day, I brought a poster board to class.

On it was a three-columned chart with the headings: Task, Teacher, and Student. The first column listed ten age appropriate concepts. I explained that we would take turns being teacher and student, giving everyone an opportunity to instruct. I wanted the children to recognize that we all learn from each other.

The Message: Learning is a lifelong process. The more I learn, the more I realize how little I know.

The Wisdom: *What does the Lord require of you? Only to do what is right and to love goodness, to walk humbly with God* (Micah 6:8).

The Action: Be open to learning something new and view everyone as a potential teacher.

HELP IS THERE, JUST ASK

"I don't feel good and I think you should write a note to my mom. It is pretty bad. So, I think you should write two notes."

It was 8:45 and the day seemed long already. Brian was at it again. He had been terrorizing the other children by taking their building blocks and throwing them and other objects, at his classmates. Alarmed and frustrated, I told Brian to take his seat immediately.

After five minutes, I told Brian to get up, apologize to the others, and pick up the scattered blocks. He did, but before long, he was poking and prodding his classmates again. Finally, I took him aside and tried to explain the right and wrong way to get attention. He just sulked, "Can I go back to my seat?" "Sure," I said, "We'll begin our phonics lesson soon anyway."

Brian took his seat, laid his head on the desktop, and placed his hands over his head. When I instructed the children to take out their phonics papers, Brian said, "I don't feel good and I think you should write a note to my mom. It's pretty bad. So, I think you should write two notes." Looking back, I laugh at the notion of two notes. How clever of Brian! He knew it was time to contact Mom and he theorized that two notes were sure to get him the attention he sought. At the time, however, I was not laughing. I was rather upset, in fact. Not because Brian was so frustrating, although his behavior was tiring, but because I couldn't fix the problem.

We teachers receive countless hours of instruction and preparation prior to entering a classroom, and then countless more as student teachers. Nonetheless, situations arise that stump us. Brian was a prime example. I knew that I did not have the answers and it was time to seek help from our counseling office.

The counselor contacted Brian's parents and learned that his behavior at home was not much better. The four of us, Brian's parents, the counselor, and I got together and developed a cooperative strategy to encourage positive behavior. We met regularly to compare notes and discuss Brian's progress. Our efforts paid off. Before long, Brian acclimated to school life and subsequently he returned to his pleasant self at home, too.

The Message: Teamwork is often the most effective work.

The Wisdom: *Give your burdens to the Lord, and He will take care of you* (Psalm 55:22).

The Action: Do not hesitate to ask for help when you need it.

SING A SIMPLE SONG

"Mrs. C is sad. Maybe we can make her feel better."

Mrs. C had promised God that if she were cured, she would dedicate the rest of her life to helping others. She had a brain tumor and the prognosis prior to surgery was not good. Mrs. C committed herself to God and her recovery was nothing shy of a medical miracle. The tumor was successfully removed and Mrs. C set about to help others.

I was one of many who reaped the benefits of Mrs. C's promise to God. As a volunteer classroom aide, she was a sheer blessing. Impeccably dressed with reading glasses dangling from the chain around her neck, and with her hair kept in a smart short style, Mrs. C was a perfect grandmother figure. She was very approachable, patient, and kind. I didn't know Mrs. C prior to her brain tumor trauma but I seriously doubt that she was any different.

No doubt, enduring such a serious illness was tough but her biggest test of this life was yet to come. She received word late one April afternoon that her thirty-seven-year-old son was killed in a car accident. Upon hearing the tragic news, another aide and I went to visit her immediately. We sat on opposite sides of Mrs. C on her living room couch, holding her hands as she quietly remembered her son. She recalled a number of stories that brought tears to our eyes and she said over and over again how he would be missed. Her sentiments were echoed by the sorrowful cries coming from her husband who was sitting in the kitchen. All we could do was squeeze her hands tighter and pray silently.

Mrs. C returned to the classroom rather quickly. She said that being with the children was therapeutic. They alleviated her heartache unlike any prescription ever could.

I had explained Mrs. C's absence to the children prior to her return. After her first day back, Carolyn came up to me, tugged on my arm, and with a twinkle in her eye, asked if we could find a way to bring Mrs. C a smile. We decided to dedicate *Sing A Simple Song* a touching tune with a moving melody to Mrs. C at our Mother's Tea. The children had been practicing sign language all year with Mrs. C. So, rather than sing the lyrics, we signed them.

Tears flowed freely as the children signed, "Oh Lord I love you, and know that you love me too." They truly put their hearts and souls into their presentation and Mrs. C was deeply touched. She later told me that whenever she began to grieve her loss, remembering the students' performance comforted her.

The Message: Like music, children play an important roll in healing.

The Wisdom: *Come to me, all you who are weary and find life burdensome, and I will refresh you* (Matthew 11:28).

The Action: Take comfort in the simple things life offers, like the unconditional love of a child.

USE YOUR IMAGINATION

"The oil level is now at 42"

One of the greatest joys of teaching Kindergarten was watching children play. Morning sessions were more structured than afternoons in my full-day class. Academic instruction occurred during the first part of the day, while math games, drawing, and coloring were usually reserved for after lunch, along with "free play." When given the choice, the children almost always opted for free play. Casually I walked around the room to monitor their activities. Their resourcefulness and creativity always astounded me.

"The oil level is now at 42," Ryan called to Timmy. The boys were auto mechanics. Timmy charted the data as Ryan worked under the hood inspecting a car.

"I hope everything is under control there," Janine said. She had made a quick phone call home to check on things before continuing her shopping.

A group of girls had put on some old clothes that were sent in for dress-up. They were waitresses serving a table of businesswomen on lunch break and a table of hungry tourists (stuffed animals that had also been dressed in the clothes.)

A supermarket took up another corner of the room. Clerks and cashiers worked diligently to meet the needs of their customers. Their shelves were stocked with food, markers, toys, and even shoes. Large signs displayed the day's "speshal valus."

Nearby, construction workers used wooden blocks to build skyscrapers, highways, and castles.

Often, the children would work together to recreate a play they had seen or to make a production out of a story we had read in class.

Everyone looked forward to free play, including me, the fly on the wall.

The Message: Creativity flourishes when the mind is at rest. Video games, TV, movies, and the Internet can over stimulate children and squelch their inventiveness. Also, too many adult-initiated organized games can dull their senses. Sometimes children have to figure it out for themselves in order to grow.

The Wisdom: *Let your heart give you joy in the days of your youth* (Ecclesiastes 11:9).

The Action: Give children plenty of down time. Resourceful adults were once very imaginative children.

THINK OF OTHERS

"I won't be in school next week because I have to go into the hospital."

Before the start of the school year, I was made aware of Karen's delicate health due to digestive problems. Although Karen almost died at birth, the prognosis for her continued improvement was good but risky. Her condition required recurrent hospitalization, which meant that she was going to miss a few weeks of school. That was not going to be a problem in my class. Having worked with five-year-olds for several years at that point, I knew that Karen's classmates would be very supportive.

Karen was a delightful student from the first day of school. She was confident, well groomed, and passionate about learning and living life to its fullest. She displayed an intense desire to make the most of every day. Her first trip to the hospital, about a month after school started, would keep her out of school for about three weeks. Karen asked the class to pray for her. Speaking earnestly, she told us that she didn't want to miss a thing, "Please save everything for me, OK?"

Not only did we pray for her, but we also checked on her with regular phone calls. The children made beautifully colored cards filled with words of concern and encouragement.

When Karen returned from her first absence, she taught her classmates and me some of the relaxation and deep breathing exercises she had learned from the nurses. During playtime one afternoon, at Karen's instruction, about ten children sat yoga-style in a row on the carpeted area of our classroom. Karen showed them how to practice deep breathing. She instructed them to think of pleasant things while they slowly inhaled and exhaled.

The room was unusually quiet as even the children who had chosen to not participate were captivated by this activity. I smiled as I watched, realizing that it would be many years before these children would come to appreciate the value of what they were learning. And to think that this was initiated by a five-year-old!

Engaging her classmates in an activity that she learned through her unfortunate situation helped Karen cope with her disease. Openly dealing with her condition was comforting to both her and her classmates.

The Message: When we give to others, we receive so much more in return.

The Wisdom: *Jesus said, "When you do something for someone else, don't call attention to yourself. When you help someone out, don't think about how it looks. Just do it—quietly and unobtrusively"* (Matthew 6:2-4).

The Action: Find a way to give of yourself.

GO WITH THE FLOW

"My dad has baby goats. Can we show the class?"

Wow! What a terrific learning opportunity a farmer with live animals could provide. And we wouldn't have to go through the expense and trouble of planning a field trip. This seemed too good to be true.

With a class of thirty, careful instruction and preparation were going to be key to the success of this show-and-tell. After receiving permission from the school principal, I set in motion plans for a smooth and brief visit from Steve's father, Farmer Keller. I firmly instructed my students to remain seated and listen while Farmer Keller informed us about goats. I told the children that if they had questions they were to politely raise their hands so that Farmer Keller could call on them one at a time, just as I do in class. I wanted to be sure that the "kids" would behave well for the kids, and vice versa. In retrospect, it may have helped if I had informed Mr. Keller about my intentions.

The livestock show-and-tell day had come. After just settling the children in their seats following morning recess, I turned toward the classroom door to find Farmer Keller standing proudly with a big grin on his friendly face. Behind the husky man sat three innocent young goats in a red wagon. As I introduced Farmer Keller, I told him that the children had been anticipating his visit and that they were ready to learn all he had to share.

As if he was being called to "come on down" on The Price Is Right, Farmer Keller took to the front of the room with swift enthusiasm. To my surprise, he invited the children to "come on down" and see the goats. I thought my heart was going to jump out of my chest. Before I could utter a word of protest, the children stormed the front of the room unwittingly scaring the goats. The animals leaped out of the wagon and ran about the classroom. Attempting to be helpful, the children ran after the goats in hopes of catching at least one.

I never felt so out of control. All I could think to do was flick the lights on and off to try to restore order. It worked. With the children settled back at their seats, Farmer Keller was able to round up the tiny animals. We thanked him for his visit and I graciously asked him to leave. He smiled and obliged. I stepped toward my teacher's aide and whispered, "Warn the Second Grade teacher to think twice about allowing the goats today."

As I paused to catch my breath and consider my next step, the children began to giggle. The laughter was contagious. In no time, I figured out why. Messy goat droppings were scattered about the room. It was as though the goats had planned my next step for me. We did not have a janitor so I had to think quickly. I told the children to remain at their seats while I grabbed sawdust from our broom closet and spread it over the muck. Doing so enabled me to sweep up the mess. I then had to scrub the affected areas with cleaning solution. This took a fair amount of time, but my students were most cooperative. The clean-up show-and-tell was a bonus lesson.

When the ordeal was over, I suggested story time. We decided to learn about goats from a book.

The Message: Life is full of the unexpected.

The Wisdom: *Trust me, o God, and know my thoughts; see whether I step in the wrong path, and guide me along the everlasting way* (Psalm 138:23-24).

The Action: Go with the flow.

SPEND TIME WITH THE SPECIAL PEOPLE IN YOUR LIFE

"Is it ok if I stay home from school tomorrow and be with my dad? Maybe we could fly a kite."

At the end of another productive day of learning, I walked down the main school hall with Danny to help him find the dismissal line for his bus route. We walked briskly and quietly, each of us exhausted after a long day and each carrying the weight of our respective duties on our shoulders. Out of nowhere, Danny blurted out, "Is it ok if I stay home from school tomorrow and be with my dad? Maybe we could fly a kite."

The innocence of Danny's question sent me into deep thought. What a crazy busy world we live in today. Wouldn't it be nice to simply spend time with loved ones doing nothing in particular?

My mother had my three siblings and me in less than five years, so our house always seemed chaotic. I remember the immense enjoyment visits from my grandmother (Nan) brought. Her visits were a break from the norm. When Nan was over, I wanted the world to stop—especially school. She'd stay with us when my parents had to go out for an evening and when Mom accompanied Dad on short business trips.

We nicknamed Nan "Sergeant York," combining her personality with her hometown, York, Pennsylvania. According to my father, Nan made us, her grand-soldiers, toe the same line he had toed. Nan reinforced the values of cleanliness and orderliness that my parents had instilled in us. And we loved her for it. Hard working and extremely fastidious, Nan was the type of woman who would rip out and then re-attach the sleeves on a store-bought blouse just to create a better fit. She was very careful to avoid spoiling her grandchildren, too. Always armed with a supply of chewing gum, Nan rationed a half stick at a time.

I relished spending time with Nan. She kept us entertained with stories about our father's childhood. We listened intently as she described the time Dad's friends waited and watched impatiently as he scrubbed the front porch on his knees. The porch was his Saturday chore, and he was not permitted to play before his chores were complete—a rule to which we could relate since Dad passed it onto us. Looking back, chore time was family time, and family time was key to my happy childhood.

The older we get, the more difficult it is to escape the rigors of everyday life. Thinking to myself that Danny could very well afford to miss a day of Kindergarten and that the benefits of spending the day with his father would be so much greater, I simply smiled at him and said nothing. I watched Danny as he got in line with the children from various grades to board his bus and I wondered how many of the children felt overwhelmed by the demands of school, after school activities, and parents' busy schedules. It's a marvel that a five-year-old could tap into such deep desire for tranquility. Clearly, something is not quite right in our fast-paced culture.

The Message: Time we spend with loved ones is special. We never get that time back.

The Wisdom: *Love begins at home.* –Mother Teresa

The Action: Make it a point each week to spend time with and learn something from a family member.

CARE ABOUT OUR WORLD

"My dad has a tree farm. Maybe our class could come and see it. My dad can plant a tree outside the classroom and then we can feed the birds."

Children are always so eager to share their worlds with the class, and Stephanie had given me a good idea. I contacted her father who indeed owned a tree farm (in his backyard) and was more than willing to conduct a tour for us. So I arranged a field trip to Stephanie's house.

Prior to the trip, we read a bit in school about the variety of trees that grow in our region and we identified the many things that are made from trees. So, by the day of our excursion, the children were eager to learn more and to see trees at various stages of growth.

Stephanie's parents, the Penna's, greeted us as we got off the bus in front of their house. Mr. Penna led us through the front door, down the main hall into the kitchen, where the children left their lunch pails, and right through the backyard and into the tree farm. Like a tour guide, Mr. Penna identified trees and shrubs as we walked passed them. We learned about the growth process. We learned about evergreens and deciduous trees. We even learned about the advantages to cutting down some trees and to leaving others grow to their full potential.

Mr. Penna graciously answered a barrage of questions, including some that were clearly beyond the inquisitors' very comprehension.

After walking up and down rows of trees and stopping frequently to study bark, leaves, and some nuts, we were ready for lunch. Mrs. Penna had spread blankets on the lawn at the clearing near the farm's entrance so that we could sit comfortably outside. The children loved this. All the chatter between bites of peanut butter and jelly or ham and cheese was about trees, oxygen, log cabins, firewood, birds, and so on.

The following school day was interrupted by the sound of a diesel engine outside. Looking out the window to see what kind of mammoth truck arrived, the children were surprised to see an evergreen emerging from the back of an oversized pick-up truck. It was Mr. Penna. I knew immediately what was going on, so I gave the children permission to get out of their seats and go to the window to watch.

Mr. Penna hopped out of his truck and began digging a hole near the schoolyard. The children cheered as he carefully shimmied the tree into the hole. "Hey, Steph," one little boy called out, "you're dad's strong!" Then, looking at the newly planted tree, we said a prayer of thanks for the gift of nature and all of its benefits.

A week later we made snacks for the birds. Using cookie cutters, we formed white bread into shapes, spread peanut butter on the bread, and then sprinkled birdseed on them. We punched holes in the top and strung the feeders to our new tree. Then, we watched as birds of many feathers pecked at our creation. This activity led to subsequent lessons on the many species of birds.

The Message: Take time to learn about nature. You will never stop learning something new.

The Wisdom: *What does the reign of God resemble? To what shall I liken it? It is like a mustard seed, which a man took and planted in his garden. It grew and became a large shrub and the birds of the air nestled in its branches* (Luke 13:18).

The Action: Find a way to care for the earth.

DREAM

"When I grow up, I want to be a rainbow watcher."

As an Early Childhood Development major in college, I learned that much is revealed about a child's character and personality through his artwork. As a teacher, I experienced this firsthand. So it didn't surprise me that Zach, who loved to draw rainbows, wanted to be a Rainbow Watcher. What was perplexing, though, is that I had never heard of such a vocation. I had heard the dreams of many aspiring doctors, nurses, firemen, and actresses, but Zach's desire to be a Rainbow Watcher was a first.

Because rainbows represent euphoria, I surmised that like most adults, Zach longed for peace. I expected the other children to inquire about the title "Rainbow Watcher," but they didn't. Instead, they appeared to understand the profession as well as the duties that went along with it, and they relished the concept of living in total contentment.

I considered my "rainbow" place: a wondrous thousand-acre botanical garden with woodlands, meadows, and fountains that's just a short drive from my home. I frequent these gardens on fair weather days and the conservatory during the colder months. These gardens reflect the brilliant colors and textures of every season. Regardless the time of year or time of day, I find peace and tranquility there.

It's so refreshing to watch people of all ages absorb the beauty of sunlight reflecting on ponds, birds cascading from branch to branch, and acre upon acre of meticulously cultivated landscape. Every sight and sound reveals the true nature of God's magnificent creation. My grandmother said it best when she remarked that such pure splendor is a glimpse of Heaven.

The Message: Dreams offer a sense of security and comfort.

The Wisdom: *Where your pleasure is, there is your treasure. Where you treasure is, there is your heart. Where your heart is, there is your happiness.* –St. Augustine

The Action: Give yourself permission to dream.

GIVE FROM THE HEART

"My mom didn't have money to buy you a present, so this is my gift."

Flowers, brightly decorated packages, and cards poured over my desk on the last day of school. The children beamed with pride and excitement as they watched me open their teacher gifts. Each wanted to see my reaction, so I made sure that I fussed over and acknowledged each one. The opportunity to teach these children was gift enough for me. The eagerness with which they offered their presents was a bonus.

Needless to say, there was a lot of commotion during this loosely structured day. Every few minutes, I looked up from the crowd of children surrounding my desk to check on those scattered about the room. I noticed that Hannah didn't seem as cheerful as usual. She sat alone, quietly looking at a book. In a split second, she must have felt my gaze upon her. She raised her head, and when our eyes met, she quickly reached for a piece of paper and brought it to me. "My mom didn't have money to buy you a present, so this is my gift," Hannah said sheepishly. She handed me a painting that she had made with the words "I Love You" written in big bold colors. I was so touched by her gesture; my eyes filled up instantly. Fighting back the tears, I took her hands in mine, looked her in the eyes and said, "I love you, too. Hannah, I will always treasure this gift. Thank you!" And then, I gave her a hug.

Hannah was one of four children whose mother was expecting her fifth. Hannah's mother also worked full-time. During parent conferences earlier that year, she had confided that her responsibilities were overwhelming and she felt guilty about the little time she had to spend with each child, especially Hannah who, for her young age, was very mature and capable. I reassured Hannah's mom that she was doing the best she could and that her children know they are loved.

As I sat holding the painting Hannah had given me, I recalled that conversation with her mother. Indeed, Hannah was years ahead of her age for she clearly understood the message of giving from the heart.

The Message: *Every gift reveals the love of the one who gives it, and that is the most important part of the gift.* –Mother Teresa

The Wisdom: *The Lord doesn't see things the way you see them. People judge by outward appearances, but the Lord looks at the heart* (1 Samuel 16:7).

The Action: Give from the heart.

FAITH GIVES US HOPE

"Where does earth end and Heaven begin?"

I've had the good fortune of being able to attend many spiritual retreats throughout my life. One of my earliest memories is traveling to the mountains of Pittsburgh, PA with my mother, siblings, grandparents, aunts, uncles, and cousins. We crowded into the back of a van and sang God's praises during the long ride. Having migrated from the Ukraine, my grandparents sang in their native language. When we finally arrived, I was awestruck at the sight of thousands of people kneeling in prayer in a vast clearing on the side of the mountain.

Just before the turn of the century, I visited Medjugorje, Yugoslavia, not far from where my grandparents' were born. Because of government opposition to public displays of Faith, it took thirty years to build the Church in Medjugorje. Considering the amount of faith and perseverance the local townspeople had, I became filled with emotion as I stood in front of the church admiring its structure. The church bells rang as I stood there watching villagers pour in to worship at high noon. I was so moved by their devotion that I began to cry. How many of their ancestors paid the ultimate sacrifice in order to build this church?

More recently, I had a wonderful faith-sharing experience right here in the USA. I was among the thousands who went to New York City to attend Mass with Pope Benedict, XVI. Spiritual retreats are filled with graces that touch the heart and renew the spirit. There is no doubt in my mind that our God is a loving God who wants us to turn to Him, to listen, and to allow His Spirit, His peace, to enter us for we are His precious children.

Faith is believing without seeing. Faith is hope. Faith is a gift from God.

I thank God everyday for the gift of faith. So when a child innocently asked, "Where does earth end and Heaven begin?" I answered without hesitation, "Heaven is where God takes us and there will be only good things there and no more pain."

The Message: Faith gives us hope, sustains us in our needs, strengthens us, fills us with love and peace, it is our reason for living and our joy.

The Wisdom: *Those who hope in the Lord will renew their strength. They will soar on wings like Eagles; they will run and not grow weary, they will walk and not be faint* (Isaiah 40:31).

The Action: Know that you are not alone and that God, your Father, loves you.